BLOODY History of America

AMERICA'S BLOODY HISTORY FROM WORLD WAR II TO THE CIVIL RIGHTS MOVEMENT

BLOODY History of America

AMERICA'S BLOODY HISTORY FROM WORLD WAR II TO THE CIVIL RIGHTS MOVEMENT

KIERON CONNOLLY

Enslow Publishing
101 W. 23rd Street
Suite 240
New York, NY 10011
USA
enslow.com

This edition published in 2018 by

Enslow Publishing, LLC
101 W. 23rd Street, Suite 240
New York, NY 10011

Library of Congress Cataloging-in-Publication Data
Names: Connolly, Kieron, author.
Title: America's bloody history from World War II to the Civil Rights Movement / Kieron Connolly.
Description: New York, NY : Enslow Publishing, 2018. | Series: Bloody history of America | Includes bibliographical references and index. | Audience: Grades 7–12.
Identifiers: LCCN 2017031487 | ISBN 9780766091795 (library bound) | ISBN 9780766095571 (paperback)
Subjects: LCSH: United States—History—1945—Juvenile literature. | World War, 1939–1945—Juvenile literature. | Civil rights movements—United States—History 20th century—Juvenile literature. | African Americans—Civil rights—History—20th century—Juvenile literature.
Classification: LCC E741 .C575 2017 | DDC 973.91—dc23
LC record available at https://lccn.loc.gov/2017031487

Printed in China

To Our Readers: We have done our best to make sure all websites in this book were active and appropriate when we went to press. However, the author and the publisher have no control over and assume no liability for the material available on those websites or on any websites they may link to. Any comments or suggestions can be sent by email to customerservice@enslow.com.

Photo Credits: Cover (left), pp. 3 (left), 6 Everett Collection/Shutterstock.com; cover (right), p. 3 (right) Bettmann/Getty Images; Alamy: 49 (Pictorial Press), 64 (Vintageusa1); Alamy/Everett Collection: 39, 52, 62, 67, 71, 74; Alamy/Granger Collection: 20, 60; Cody Images: 21; Getty Images: 38 (Hulton), 41 (Michael Ochs Archive), 47 (Hulton), 53 (Universal Images Group), 56 (Flip Schulke Archives), 58 (Hulton), 78 (Fed W. McDarrah); Getty Images/Archive Photos: 13, 37, 65, 66, 73; Getty Images/Bettmann: 15, 34, 48, 70, 76; Library of Congress: 10 (Dorothea Lange), 42, 45; US Department of Defense: 9, 12, 14, 16, 22, 24, 26–31 all.

CONTENTS

The mid-twentieth century included years of war and involved the deployment of soldiers from all over the world to many different countries. The United States was a major player in these conflicts, with key roles in both World War II and the Korean War.

INTRODUCTION

THE HISTORY OF THE UNITED STATES IS A COMPLEX ONE, EVEN FOR a country that is still so young in the context of the world. The growth of the United States has been characterized by so many distinct periods, some of which even seemed to conflict with each other. For instance, even though the United States fought alongside their international Allies in World War II and eventually helped determine the peace terms to end the war, segregation and racial tensions, which sometimes provoked riots and other instances of violence, still existed within the United States itself.

World War II ended, but the Cold War and the Korean War soon followed, drawing more US attention and resources. Even though the United States had become a superpower and was so involved on the world stage, it remained vulnerable at home in certain ways. The fear of communism brought on by the Cold War, for instance, was molded by people like Senator Joe McCarthy, and led to the unfair treatment of many citizens, whether they were associated with communism or not.

Marginalized groups, specifically African Americans, began to speak out more strongly against the unjust divisions in the American population. Leaders like Martin Luther King Jr. called for the end of segregation and worked tirelessly for voting rights for African Americans. Activist groups flourished during the civil rights movement, and even though they didn't always agree, their accomplishments were only the beginning of a more peaceful and equal America.

CHAPTER 1

WORLD WAR II

ALTHOUGH AMERICA PROCLAIMED ITS NEUTRALITY WHEN WORLD War II broke out in Europe in 1939, in just a few years it would not only be forced into the bloodiest conflict in world history, but also determine the war's outcome. Then, in 1945, it would signal the birth of the nuclear age when it dropped atomic bombs on Japan.

The United States declared war against Japan the day after the attacks on Pearl Harbor in 1941. However, America hadn't, despite its claims, been wholly neutral since the war had begun in September 1939. Although there was much anti-war sentiment in the United States, President Roosevelt was staunchly anti-fascist and was soon quietly providing Britain and France with aid and support in their fight against Adolf Hitler's Germany. Within three months of Britain and France going to war, America's Neutrality Act had been revised to permit them to buy munitions on a "cash and carry" basis. The following September, the United States gave Britain fifty aging destroyers, while making sure that this was presented as a business deal rather than aid, with Britain, in return, offering America long leases on naval bases. Similarly, by 1941, the Lend-Lease Bill pretended that vast amounts of weaponry were only being loaned to Britain and the Soviet Union—for return after use.

Domestically, rearmament had been stepped up and conscription reintroduced. "Vicariously at least," writes historian Philip Jenkins, "the United States was in all essential ways a combatant power for most of 1941." The mass raid on Pearl Harbor may have come out of the blue, but an attack of some kind had been expected, although Malaya or the

US infantrymen pose with the flag of the defeated occupying Nazi regime in a liberated part of France, August 1944. When the United States entered the war in 1941, there were fewer than two million Americans in the armed forces; by 1945, there were more than twelve million.

ATTACKS ON AMERICA

With Japanese expansion across the Pacific and attacks on US merchant shipping, fears grew of an invasion of the American West Coast. No attempt at invasion happened, but there were some isolated assaults. In February 1942, a Japanese submarine fired shells at the Ellwood Oil Field near Santa Barbara, southern California. That June, another Japanese submarine fired shells at Fort Stevens on the Columbia River in Oregon—though without causing significant damage. Three months later, the continental US saw its only air raid of the war when a floatplane launched from a submarine dropped two incendiary bombs on the mountains of Oregon. Due to poor weather and the actions of fire patrols, the fires were put out with minimal damage.

Between November 1944 and April 1945, the Japanese Navy launched more than 9,000 fire balloons towards North America. Most were ineffective, but five children and a woman were killed in Oregon when one of the children tampered with a bomb that one of the balloons had been carrying—they would be the war's only deaths in mainland America due to enemy action. Worries about traitors in the nation's midst after the attack on the Ellwood Oil Field had led to the justification of the internment of almost 120,000 Japanese-Americans in mainland America—nearly two-thirds of whom were US citizens. Of course, Germany and Italy were also at war with the US, but there was no internment of the many Americans from German or Italian families. As the proportion of Japanese-Americans in Hawaii was too large for mass internment, martial law was imposed on the islands instead.

However, a number of Japanese-Americans from Hawaii, some of whom had been in the Hawaii National Guard, successfully petitioned to be allowed to serve in the US armed forces, and in 1943 the 442nd Infantry Regimental Combat Team of Japanese-American soldiers was formed. Generally forbidden from front-line action in the Pacific War, some used their language skills in intelligence work, while others fought in Europe. In total, about 14,000 men served with the 442nd. With 9,486 Purple Heart military honors awarded, it became, considering its size, the most decorated unit in the war.

Japanese American families assembling in Turlock, California, in May 1942, before being sent to internment camps in Arizona.

Philippines had been thought more likely targets. Back in 1937, Japanese aircraft had sunk the US gunboat *Panay* while it was anchored on the Yangtze River in China, and, concerned about Japan's imperialistic expansion in China and southeast Asia, America was already offering covert aid to the Chinese war effort, including the use of American pilots. Following the sinking, commercial treaties with Japan had been annulled and economic restrictions imposed—including, crucially, access to American oil.

PEARL HARBOR

Beginning at 7:48 a.m., the attack at Pearl Harbor on December 7, 1941 consisted of two waves of 353 Japanese aircraft—fighters, bombers, and torpedo planes—launched from six aircraft carriers, which the United States had failed to spot maneuvering into range. All eight US battleships in port were damaged, with four of them sunk, while three destroyers and three cruisers were also damaged or sunk.

Within a couple of hours, 2,400 Americans were dead. Fortunately for America, its aircraft carriers were not in the base at the time and, therefore, not hit. Furthermore, six of the battleships damaged at Pearl Harbor were returned to service. Would America now join Britain in the European war against Germany? The question was swiftly resolved when Hitler declared war on the United States four days later.

ALL EIGHT BATTLESHIPS IN PORT WERE DAMAGED, WITH FOUR OF THEM SUNK.

THE PACIFIC CAMPAIGN

In the first months of the war, America's main military concern was to stop the Japanese expansion across the Pacific. Malaya had fallen the day after the attack on Pearl Harbor, to be followed by the Dutch East Indies in March, and Burma and the Philippines in May. Australia, too, was threatened, with Darwin's port and airfields attacked in a large air raid in February.

The USS *Shaw* was attacked during the Japanese raids on Pearl Harbor on December 7, 1941. Within months, the destroyer had been repaired and went on to serve in the Pacific for the rest of the war.

BATAAN DEATH MARCH

With the Japanese advancing in the Philippines, as many as seventy-six thousand starving American and Filipino soldiers were caught in Bataan province. Surrendering in April 1942, they were forced to march 60 miles (97 kilometers), before being transported by train to a prison camp. Some died of hunger or dysentery in the cramped, unsanitary conditions on the trains or at the prison camp. Others, regarded by the Japanese as subhuman for having surrendered,

SOME DIED OF HUNGER OR DYSENTERY IN THE CRAMPED, UNSANITARY CONDITIONS.

were beaten, bayoneted, and even beheaded on the march—between seven thousand and ten thousand POWs were killed.

After the war, Masaharu Homma, the military commander of the Philippines during the Japanese occupation, was tried as a war criminal and executed, along with seven other senior-ranking soldiers.

TURNING THE TIDE IN THE PACIFIC

In May 1942, America reasserted itself in the Pacific with its first major victory at the Battle of the Coral Sea. This also marked a change in warfare: it was the first battle in which aircraft carriers engaged each other

American prisoners of war in Bataan in the Philippines in 1942. Shortly afterward, they were marched 60 miles (97 km) by the Japanese to a prison camp, with many POWs dying en route from exhaustion or disease. Others were executed.

A US Navy aircraft attacks Japanese ships at the Battle of Midway in June 1942. With the sinking of all four of Japan's large aircraft carriers, the battle was a major turning point in the war in the Pacific.

through their aircraft, but where the ships neither directly sighted nor fired on each other. Battleships would become a thing of the past, and future naval battles would be led by aircraft carriers.

The following month saw an even more significant victory for the United States. The Japanese had hoped to lure the American fleet into a trap at Midway Atoll—located, as its name suggests, halfway across the Pacific. But American cryptographers had learned the planned date of the Japanese attack, and, instead, the United States was able

SABOTEURS

As Germany didn't openly attack the American homeland, what was U-boat *U-202* doing less than 656 feet (200 m) from the Long Island shore one morning in June 1942? The answer: It was part of a bizarre sabotage mission.

That day, *U-202* and another U-boat in Florida each dropped a team of four German agents at the American coast. The agents, who had all lived in America at some point before the war, were on missions to blow up power stations and factories. But, with only two months of intelligence training, their secret operation soon began to unravel. The four agents from *U-202* made it to the beach in an inflatable raft, but within minutes they were discovered by coast guard John Cullen. When challenged, the leader of the saboteurs, George John Dasch, claimed that they were fishermen, grabbed Cullen, and stuffed $260 into his hand, hoping to buy Cullen's silence.

Outnumbered, Cullen left the men and went to inform his colleagues. In the meantime, the agents took the train to New York City, where they checked into a hotel. Six days later, and before attempting to sabotage anything, Dasch turned himself in to the authorities.

With Dasch's information, the FBI quickly rounded up the remaining agents across the country. None had yet attempted any sabotage. As Dasch and another agent, Ernst Peter Burger, had cooperated, they escaped the death penalty, receiving long prison sentences and being deported after the war. The remaining six would-be saboteurs were sent to the electric chair.

According to Hitler's architect, Albert Speer, the Führer was intoxicated by the idea of "the downfall of New York in towers of flames," but with America so far from German-occupied Europe, this failed operation would be the only attempt of its kind.

Coast Guardsman John Cullen (*left*) receives the Legion of Merit for raising the alarm after encountering German spies on the Long Island shore.

to surprise the Japanese fleet. In the battle, all four of Japan's large aircraft carriers and a heavy cruiser were sunk, while the United States lost one aircraft carrier and a destroyer. More than three hundred Americans were killed, but the Japanese lost ten times as many. Midway would be the turning point in American fortunes in the Pacific War.

Preparations for the Allied invasion of Europe. Tanks are boarded onto American landing craft at a naval base in Tunisia, before the assault on Sicily in July 1943.

THE MEDITERRANEAN THEATER

American ground troops based in Europe first saw action in November 1942, when British and US forces broadened the Allied campaign in North Africa by landing in Morocco and Algeria. Six months later, the Allies had succeeded in pushing German forces out of North Africa, but it was already too late to prepare for a major invasion of German-occupied France that year, which was the priority. Instead, the Mediterranean was chosen as the point of assault, with the aim of knocking out Italy and approaching the German lines from the south.

Beginning in July 1943, Sicily was invaded with a major airborne and amphibious operation by US, British, Canadian, Free French, Australian and South African troops against Italian and German forces. Within six weeks, the island had been taken, allowing Allied shipping to resume in the Mediterranean. Also, in late July, a coup deposed Italian dictator Benito Mussolini, and the Italian government, though openly continuing the war, secretly began to approach the Allies about reaching a peace agreement. In September, the Allies attacked the Italian mainland; within a month, the whole of southern Italy was in Allied hands—at which point their advance slowed. In January 1944, American-led Allied forces made an amphibious landing in Anzio, 29 miles (46 km) south of Rome, with the intention of outflanking the German defensive line across Italy and occupying the capital. They were eventually successful in this, but it took them 136 days, with the Allies pinned down on the marshes of Anzio for much of the time. The battle cost the Allies seven thousand lives, with thirty-six thousand wounded or missing. Two days after occupying Rome, the Italian campaign became of secondary importance—the Allied invasion of France had finally been launched.

BOMBING FROM BRITAIN

From mid-1942, US bombers based in Britain launched raids across occupied Europe, targeting military positions, munitions factories, industrial sites, ports, and railways in Germany, where the additional aim was to lower civilian morale, as well as in occupied France and the Netherlands. With America raiding by day and the British by night, the talk was of "precision bombing," but it was estimated that only 20 percent of bombs fell within 1,000 feet (300 m) of their targets.

Most controversially, on the night of February 13 to 14, 1945, 722 British Lancaster bombers targeted the city of Dresden with high explosive bombs and incendiary devices. The following day, 527 American B-17 bombers took over the raid. The bombing and resulting firestorm destroyed about 60 percent of the inner city, killing twenty-five thousand people. Seventy years later, the merits of the attack are still debated, with many arguing that the cultural city had no strategic value and was targeted when it was clear that Germany was going to lose the war. Defenders of the action, however, claim that it was a major rail transport and communication center, with 110 factories and fifty thousand workers contributing to the German war effort.

Not that life for bomber aircrews was without risk; quite the opposite. The 10-man crew on a B-17 "Flying Fortress" had a one-in-four chance of completing their tour of twenty-five missions before they could return to America—until the odds worsened in 1944, when a tour of duty was extended to thirty missions. By the end of the war, the United States Army Air Forces had lost almost ten thousand bomber aircraft, eight thousand fighter aircraft, and almost eighty thousand personnel.

OPERATION OVERLORD

By the time it came to the Allied invasion of France in June 1944, America was producing 40 percent of the world's armaments and an American,

General Dwight Eisenhower, was leading the Allied armed forces. The United States had entered the war late, but it was now the senior partner in investment, armament, and manpower in the Anglo-American alliance.

Germany anticipated an Allied amphibious attack on occupied France, but thought that it would probably be in Pas de Calais—the nearest crossing point from Britain. Consequently, this area was particularly well defended. Instead, the Allies chose Normandy, farther southwest and less well armed. However, as surprise was hugely important, bombing raids targeting transport links and supply columns were made not just in Normandy, but across France, so as not to give away the chosen location of the invasion.

D-DAY

Just before midnight on June 5, 1944, 1,200 aircraft departed England to transport airborne divisions of US, British, and Free French troops to their drop zones behind enemy lines in France. Naval bombardments began at 5:45 a.m. the following morning, with the first infantry landing craft reaching the five target beaches 45 minutes later. The beach landings were led by American, British, and Canadian forces, with Polish, Norwegian, Free French, and Dutch forces also involved. On that day, June 6, 1944, 132,000 Allied men were transported by sea to the beaches and a further 24,000 parachuted into Normandy or landed by glider.

The aim for the first day had been to advance 6 to 10 miles (10–16 km) inland, four of the beachheads to link up, and a number of towns, including Caen, to be taken. None of these objectives was achieved and it would take two months to occupy Caen. Nevertheless, the beaches themselves were secured. Allied casualties on the first day were at least 10,000, with 4,414 confirmed dead; the Germans lost 1,000 men. But, although slowly at first, the Allied troops soon began pushing out from the beaches. The Normandy landings remain the largest seaborne invasion in history, involving nearly 5,000 landing and assault craft, 289 escort vessels and

Detroit factories employed southern blacks in the war effort. But with the city short of housing, race riots erupted.

277 minesweepers. Before Operation Overlord was completed, more than one million Allied troops would land in France.

SEGREGATION AND DISCRIMINATION

The war pulled the United States out of the Depression, and the flow of black people in the South moving north for work resumed. Racial discrimination remained, however, and with the surge of migrants into Detroit, Michigan, competing for jobs and homes, race riots broke out there in the summer of 1943. Rioting raged for three days, leading to the deaths of thirty-four people, most of whom were black.

Discrimination hadn't ended in the armed forces, either. Black people still served in segregated units and more often in noncombatant roles, such as trucking and construction. They were housed in poorer accommodations and were restricted from some bars and restaurants. They could serve their country, but might not be served *in* their country.

Once abroad, however, it was a different experience. In Britain, Italy, and France there was no formal racial ban, so black people were largely free to go where they pleased. But what then would life be like for them on their return to America? With the end of the war, many

NATIVE AMERICANS

Although not permitted to vote in many states, the US government required all Native American men to register for military conscription. Many refused: the Seminole declared that they were still at war with the US, while the Iroquois objected because they didn't consider themselves to be American citizens. Still, one-third of all eligible Indian males and around 800 Indian women joined the armed forces to serve in the war.

In addition to their combat role, Native Americans proved particularly useful in secret communications. The US Marines established the Navajo code talker unit of around 400 men, where the bilingual soldiers devised a code in Navajo for use in radio communications—a code the Japanese never managed to crack. A similar approach was taken by Comanche and Choctaw soldiers.

Navajo-speaking soldiers make encrypted radio communications during the Pacific islands' campaign. The Japanese never managed to crack the code used by the Navajos.

BLACKS COULD SERVE THEIR COUNTRY, BUT MIGHT NOT BE SERVED *IN* THEIR COUNTRY.

African-Americans dreaded the return to segregated life at home. Although that would be the case, the war years also loosened up social mobility by removing a large proportion of the young male population from the work force, which allowed women and African-Americans to fill roles that had previously been blocked to them.

The D-Day landings, June 6, 1944. American soldiers are pulled ashore after their landing craft was sunk by enemy action off Utah Beach, Normandy, France.

FROM NORMANDY TO GERMANY

In August 1944, around fifty thousand German soldiers were cut off when the British and Americans managed to encircle them south of Caen in what has become known as the Falaise Pocket. From there, the Allies could approach Paris, completing the liberation of the French capital on August 23. By September they were in Belgium; in October, the first German city, Aachen, fell.

But then in December came the German counteroffensive, pushing the Allied lines 60 miles (100 km) back into Belgium. Referred to as the Battle of the Bulge for the way the Germans "bulged" back into the Allied lines, the German advance through the Ardennes forest caught the Allies by surprise. Eventually, though, Allied heavy bombers were able to target German troops and supply lines, weakening enemy fuel and ammunition supplies. From there, the Allies steadily pushed the exhausted Germans back into Germany.

THE HOLOCAUST

The all-black 761st Tank Battalion was among the American forces that liberated the Nazi concentration camp at Buchenwald, near Weimar in Germany in April 1945. For inmate Ben Bender, a seventeen-year-old Polish Jew, these were the first black faces he had ever seen. But there was another surprise for Bender: "I could not understand why people wielding arms and steel would have tears in their eyes," he said, when interviewed by the *New York Times* almost fifty years later. "In Buchenwald people didn't cry. They moaned, like wounded animals." Weeping at the sight of twenty thousand emaciated prisoners, the soldiers helped where they could, although more than two thousand prisoners were too weak to be saved. Probably more than forty-two thousand people had already died at the camp from shootings,

IN BUCHENWALD PEOPLE DIDN'T CRY. THEY MOANED, LIKE WOUNDED ANIMALS.

For the first time in the war, Americans met serious Japanese opposition to an amphibious landing when US Marines came ashore on the beaches of Tarawa in 1943.

In May 1945, the aircraft carrier USS *Bunker Hill* was attacked by two kamikazes, causing a huge fire. Casualties exceeded 600, with 346 confirmed dead.

RAISING THE FLAG AT IWO JIMA

Closer to the Japanese home islands, Iwo Jima, a small volcanic island situated halfway between Tokyo and the Mariana Islands, was targeted in February 1945. Successive aerial bombardments since 1944 had not significantly affected the Japanese defenses, which involved a massive

The city of Nagasaki after the dropping of the atomic bomb on August 9, 1945. At least thirty-five thousand people were killed and sixty thousand others injured by the bomb, with more deaths following from the long-term effects of radiation.

network of hidden guns and bunkers. On February 19, the Japanese waited until thirty thousand US Marines had landed on the beaches, before opening fire, killing or wounding two thousand men before the end of the day. Four days of fighting later, the Marines reached the summit of Mount Suribachi, raising the Stars and Stripes flag there on February 23. The photograph of this moment would become a symbol of American valor in the war.

It would be another month, however, before the island was finally secured. Again, casualties were very high, with Japanese losses in excess of 20,000 and only 1,083 prisoners taken—the rest having fought to the death. The Marines lost 6,800 men, with nearly 20,000 wounded. With such high losses, it remains a matter of debate among historians whether Iwo Jima was strategically worth the casualties sustained.

KAMIKAZES AT OKINAWA

The largest amphibious assault in the Pacific War came at Okinawa in April 1945. A large island only 340 miles (550 km) from mainland Japan, Okinawa would, it was planned, be used as a base for later US air operations against the Japanese home islands. Before that, however, attacks on American naval vessels, many by suicidal Kamikaze pilots, caused 4,900 American deaths and the loss of 38 ships, while inland 75,000 US soldiers were wounded or killed in the fighting. Before the island was finally captured, 94 percent of 110,000 Japanese soldiers stationed there—along with many civilians—were killed defending it.

THE ATOMIC BOMB

Despite huge Japanese military losses as the Americans neared Japan's home islands, and the firestorms caused by US bombing of the largely wooden houses of the enemy's cities, demands for an unconditional surrender were still being refused. There had been an immense cost in American lives in taking the Pacific islands, and it was now estimated that invading Japan itself could result in the deaths of at least another forty thousand Americans. On top of that there was concern that an invasion might provoke Japanese revenge attacks on Allied POWs.

While the war had been going on, the secret Manhattan Project had developed two usable atomic bombs. After weighing up all these considerations, President Harry S. Truman (having succeeded Roosevelt, who had died of a stroke that April) took the decision, with the consent of Britain, to drop an atomic bomb on the city of Hiroshima on August 6. Although a major industrial city with a large military garrison, a bomb of that size inevitably also caused mainly civilian casualties.

When Japan still didn't surrender, a second bomb was dropped on Nagasaki, a major seaport, three days later. On the same day, the Soviet Union entered the Pacific War. Japan finally gave in, and a formal ceremony of surrender was performed on board the USS *Missouri* in Tokyo Bay on September 2. World War II was over. At least 129,000 people were killed by the two atomic bombs, roughly half on the day each bomb fell. During the following months, many more died from the effects of burns and radiation sickness, exacerbated by malnutrition. The moral debate continues. Were the nuclear attacks on Hiroshima and Nagasaki justified in that they brought the war to a close? Or were they war crimes?

AT LEAST 129,000 PEOPLE WERE KILLED BY THE TWO ATOMIC BOMBS.

COUNTING THE COST

More than 16 million Americans served in the armed forces during the war, of whom 292,000 died in battle and 114,000 from other causes. Including civilians, German losses were between five and eight million, while Japanese losses were up to three million. Counting military and

The end of World War II. The Japanese surrender delegation on board the USS *Missouri* in Tokyo Bay on September 2, 1945.

civilian deaths in all countries involved, more than 60 million people died in the war.

What had been achieved was the crushing of brutal Japanese imperialism in the Pacific, the removal of Italian fascism and the destruction of a genocidal German fascist regime that had conquered most of Europe.

THE NEW SUPERPOWERS

America ended World War II as the greatest economic and military power in the world—the first superpower. The only nation with the potential to challenge it was the communist Soviet Union. United against the common foe of fascism, the United States and the Soviet Union had been allies during the fighting, but even before the conflict ended, the relationship between the two was breaking down into a war of a different kind.

CHAPTER 2

THE EARLY COLD WAR

WORLD WAR II HAD LEFT EUROPE EXHAUSTED, AND THE WARTIME alliance between the Allies would quickly disintegrate. Internationally, American troops would see action opposing the expansion of communism, while at home the country would hunt down communists—both real and imagined.

In 1945, the Allies, led by the United States, the Soviet Union, and Britain, decided the peace terms to end World War II. That October, the same three countries became the founding members of the United Nations. Yet, only three years later, President Truman would scribble to his Secretary of State, George Marshall, "Will Russia move first? Who pulls the trigger? Then where do we go?" Much was changing in international relations—and very quickly.

Rather than a peaceful period of gradual reconstruction, by the summer of 1945 the victors were already haggling over the peace. Now that the old enemy of German fascism was out of the way, the vast differences between the capitalist democracies and Soviet communism reemerged.

Supporters praise Senator Joseph McCarthy while he was facing censure charges in 1954. The name most associated with the anticommunist purges of the 1940s and 1950s, McCarthy—and his rabble-rousing methods—stirred the paranoia of Cold War America.

The Soviet Union didn't retire to prewar boundaries, but, instead, installed communist governments across Eastern Europe, thus reneging on a promise to allow free elections. It was as early as March 1946 that Winston Churchill uttered the words, "from Stettin in the Baltic to Trieste in the Adriatic, an iron curtain has descended across the continent."

DIVIDING GERMANY

The fate of Germany encapsulated the struggles between East and West. After the war, the country was to be shared by the Allies, with British, French, and American forces occupying the West and the Soviet Union taking the East. But Berlin, the capital, was far in the east, so the city was divided like a mini version of the whole nation, with British, French, and American zones in the western part of the city, and the Russian sector in the eastern part. That settled the borders for the time being, but how was the country to be reconstructed? And what kind of economic system or government would it have? That was undecided.

SUPPORTING GREECE

Previously isolationist, the two World Wars had proved to America the interdependency of nations. Wary of how far Stalin hoped to expand Soviet influence by diplomacy or coercion, the United States now felt that supporting independence in Europe was in the national interest in the longer run.

When Britain, in economic crisis, was unable to support anticommunist forces in Greece in 1947, Truman presented his case to Congress: "Totalitarian regimes imposed upon free people, by direct and indirect aggression, undermine the foundations of international peace and hence the security of the United States…." The speech, which became known as the Truman Doctrine, depicted the world on the brink of falling either towards freedom or totalitarianism—by which it was understood he meant communism. Persuaded, Congress agreed for aid to be sent to Greece.

THE MARSHALL PLAN

Across war-torn Europe, US Secretary of State George Marshall witnessed the poverty and slow recovery of the continent and concluded that the area was ripe to fall prey to communism. To avoid such an eventuality, Marshall proposed an aid program—the Marshall Plan—to revive "a working economy in the world so as to permit the emergence of political and economic conditions in which free institutions can exist."

As this would involve opening up Soviet satellite states to free-market economics, Stalin soon pulled out of the discussions, but from 1948 to 1952, the US provided $13 billion of aid to Western Europe. In the same period, the Soviet Union drained roughly the same amount from Eastern Europe.

Such was the anxiety regarding the Soviet Union that, in March 1948, Truman even asked Congress to reintroduce peacetime conscription, arguing that since the end of World War II, "the Soviet Union and its agents have destroyed the independence and democratic character of a whole series of nations in eastern and central Europe." The only other occasion peacetime conscription had been introduced was in 1940—and the country had gone to war little more than a year later.

THE BERLIN BLOCKADE

Three years after the war's end, Germany was still dependent on Allied supplies and had been reduced to a barter economy. In June 1948, the United States, Britain, and France introduced a new currency—the Deutschmark—into their German zones, which included West Berlin. Quickly, goods began appearing in West German shops again, but how did this make the East look? Stalin's response was to blockade the roads to West Berlin, cutting off supplies to that part of the city.

US military police in postwar Berlin. With the Soviet Union controlling East Berlin, the Americans, British, and French each policed a zone in West Berlin.

The first consignment of American Marshall Aid Plan sugar arrives in London in February 1949.

Already commentators were describing the broader situation between East and West as a "Cold War"—a war of nerves. Now those nerves would be tested. The West did not aggravate the situation militarily, but the Americans and British flew in aid, with, at its peak, aircraft landing every thirty seconds to supply the two million people of West Berlin. The Soviets could have escalated the situation and shot down the planes, but they didn't. The airlift lasted until May the following year, when Stalin lifted the blockade. As historian David Reynolds writes, "His bluff had been called and he had no stomach for war." A bloody situation had been averted.

Following the blockade, the Truman administration argued for the creation of the North Atlantic Treaty (later to become NATO), under which the US, Canada, and Western European countries promised loyalty to each other should one come under attack. This only reinforced the iron curtain, but the situation was already escalating farther east when, in the same year, the Soviet Union began testing atomic bombs. Meanwhile China—the world's most populous country—had come under communist control.

THE TWO WORLD WARS HAD PROVED TO AMERICA THE INTERDEPENDENCY OF NATIONS.

THE KOREAN WAR

Occupied by Japan during World War II, Korea had, like Germany, been carved up by the victors. Soviet forces had taken over northern Korea and American troops the south. The 38th Parallel, where the two armies met, became the dividing line between two political systems—the Soviets backing the communist North, America supporting the South.

Children in West Berlin watch as an American plane brings in supplies to the blockaded city in 1948. Over an eleven-month period, the United States, Britain, and other Western Allies flew more than two hundred thousand flights to supply Berlin.

Then, in June 1950, North Korea invaded the South. This took the United States by surprise. But America's response would surprise Stalin, too. Because the United States hadn't resisted the communist takeover of China, Stalin had approved North Korea's plans to control the whole of Korea, guessing, it would seem, that America would not

LAS VEGAS

"The gangsters who run the places are all urbane and charming," observed the English writer and actor Noël Coward in Las Vegas in 1955. "They are curious products of a most curious, adolescent country."

America was still, in European eyes, a young nation, and Las Vegas was a new town in a young state—Nevada only having entered the Union during the Civil War. Keen to attract outsiders, in the 1930s the Nevada authorities legalized gambling and prostitution, and offered quick divorces. Then, in 1941, mobster Meyer Lansky had sent Ben "Bugsy" Siegel to Nevada to run the Trans America Wire service—which was essential for bookmakers across the country to learn horse racing results. Siegel soon made it part of his agreement with the bookmakers that any who wanted his wire service had to give him a share of their profits. He was also, journalists Sally Denton and Roger Morris argue in their book *The Money and the Power*, still profiting from a wartime drug trade coming into the United States via Mexico.

Siegel's ambition was to build an upmarket casino in Las Vegas, which at the time was a small, unremarkable desert town. He succeeded—though he wouldn't live to enjoy the success. In December 1946, he opened the Flamingo Hotel & Casino, but already mobsters were unhappy about the sums they had invested in his lavish project. Its budget had risen from $1 million to $6 million, with rumors circulating that Siegel, or his girlfriend Virginia Hill, had been skimming money off the construction costs. Although by the following summer the Flamingo was already showing a profit, it was too late to save Siegel. He was shot dead at his home in Los Angeles. No one was ever tried for his murder.

Las Vegas, however, lived on. Others casinos, often backed by Mormon bankers, followed the Flamingo's success. During the 1950s, the city's population tripled to more than sixty-five thousand and there

get involved. But, remembering where unchecked aggression of 1930s' dictatorships had led, Truman felt, "if South Korea was allowed to fall Communist, leaders would be emboldened to override nations closer to our own."

IN JUNE 1950, NORTH KOREA TOOK THE US BY SURPRISE AND INVADED SOUTH KOREA.

were enough casino jobs to employ seventeen thousand people. Starry names, such as Ella Fitzgerald, Judy Garland, and Frank Sinatra, performed there. On the surface it all seemed legal, but the Kefauver Committee of 1950–51—a Senate investigation into interstate crime—was well aware of the city's links to organized crime. Authors Denton and Morris claim that Meyer Lansky, still laundering drug money through Vegas, was behind most of the casinos on the Vegas Strip, and that $3 million was being skimmed for every $1 million reported in the casinos—the undeclared income finding its way into Swiss bank accounts.

For all its gaudy charm, by the end of the decade, Las Vegas was employing three times as many police as any other city of its size, and Nevada had the highest crime and suicide rates in America.

The Rat Pack—Frank Sinatra, Dean Martin, Sammy Davis Jr., Peter Lawford, and Joey Bishop—outside Las Vegas's Sands Hotel in 1962.

With the Soviet Union boycotting the United Nations at that time, Truman was able to win UN support for US-led troops to be committed to South Korea. In September, General Douglas MacArthur landed behind enemy lines at the port of Inchon. Soon Seoul, the southern capital, was back in Allied hands. Emboldened,

Ethel and Julius Rosenberg wait in a prison van in March 1951 after being found guilty of spying for the Soviet Union. Two years later they were sent to the electric chair.

MacArthur pushed into North Korea, capturing the capital Pyongyang and ignoring warnings from China not to advance any nearer their border. The result was that on November 25, 1950, the UN soldiers were overrun by thousands of Chinese soldiers. Unprepared, the UN soldiers fled and the front line was pushed back south again, past the 38th Parallel. For a time, Seoul was in Chinese hands. When MacArthur openly proposed invading China he was dismissed from the whole conflict. Instead, the war dragged on into a stalemate until a ceasefire was agreed in 1953. The borders were returned to where they had been at the start—the 38th Parallel. In total, the US participation had involved 5.7 million men and women, with 34,000 American soldiers killed in battle.

UNPREPARED FOR THE CHINESE ATTACK, THE UN SOLDIERS WERE OVERRUN AND FLED.

THE RED SCARE

During the war, US Army code-breakers had intercepted cables between Moscow and the Soviet embassy in Washington, and found that 349 Americans had been in secret communication with Soviet agents. Among others, the evidence incriminated scientist Klaus Fuchs, who had passed details of the American atomic test to the Soviet Union, thus allowing them to develop their own bomb. He eventually admitted his guilt, was imprisoned and later emigrated to East Germany. Then there was Julius Rosenberg, who had been fired from the US Army when it was discovered that he had been a member of the Communist Party. The evidence revealed that Rosenberg was the leader of a Soviet spy ring, and that he and his wife, Ethel, had also passed information about the atomic bomb to the Soviet Union. The couple were tried and executed in the electric chair in June 1953.

Considering that these high-profile cases occurred at the same time as a rise in East-West tensions and labor unrest during the 1940s—three million workers were on strike in early 1946—it was perhaps unsurprising that the belief took hold that there were communist plots afoot in America. Truman gave the FBI, under J. Edgar Hoover, license to investigate federal employees, although the president soon balked when it was found that Hoover's FBI was "dabbling in sex life scandals and plain blackmail when they should be catching criminals."

In public life, the chairman of the House of Representatives's House Committee on Un-American Activities (HUAC), J. Parnell Thomas, was convinced by 1947 that strikes at movie studios were being inspired by communism and that films were being used to spread communist propaganda. HUAC targeted Hollywood, issuing subpoenas to actors and filmmakers to be quizzed about their political affiliations and those of others in their community.

The following year, the Communist Party leadership was found guilty of trying to overthrow the government, although it had taken no steps to achieve this beyond circulating books and pamphlets advocating such behavior. By 1951, however, many states had banned the operation of the Communist Party and had placed restrictions on its members, including, in some cases, the removal of welfare benefits. Most states also introduced loyalty oaths for public employees, requiring them to swear that they did not support any subversive causes. Major industries were targeted, too, and radical unions, such as the United Electrical Workers. University professors and teaching unions also came under suspicion. As a consequence, a wave of paranoia swept through the education system, with schools and colleges racing to purge their text books of anything that might be considered politically suspect.

SENATOR MCCARTHY

In 1950, Republican Senator Joe McCarthy of Wisconsin escalated the "reds under the beds" scare, warning in one of many apocalyptical speeches of "a final all-out battle between Communistic atheism and

MCCARTHY WARNED OF "A FINAL ALL-OUT BATTLE BETWEEN COMMUNISTIC ATHEISM AND CHRISTIANITY."

Convinced that strikes at movie studios were part of a communist plot in Hollywood, J. Parnell Thomas, chair of the House Committee on Un-American Activities (HUAC), began targeting the filmmaking industry in 1947.

TRAMPING ON CHAPLIN

Despite compiling a file 2,000 pages long, the FBI never found any evidence that Charlie Chaplin was a communist, but he had defended the civil liberties of communists and during World War II had been outspoken that the US should help the Soviet Union. For this, he attracted powerful enemies.

When 22-year-old would-be actress Joan Barry filed a paternity suit against Chaplin, the federal authorities escalated the case, indicting the star in 1944 under the Mann Act—a seldom-used statute dusted down when they wanted to harass someone—which held that it was a federal crime to transport a woman across a state line for immoral purposes. Although blood tests proved that Chaplin was not the father of Joan Barry's child, he *had* paid for her rail fare to New York, where he had met her. During his trial, the prosecution attacked Chaplin as a "master mechanic in the art of seduction." Despite the scientific evidence, he lost the paternity case and was forced to pay child support. That was a blow to the comedian's name, although the financial cost wouldn't hurt him too much.

Like many Hollywood figures, however, Chaplin wasn't American. Although the London-born comic had lived in America for forty years, making his name there, he had always retained his British passport. This would now be used against him. While he was abroad in 1953, his opponents saw their opportunity and his reentry permit was rescinded. A Justice Department spokesman cited the clause that foreigners might be barred on grounds of "morals, health, or insanity, or for advocating Communism or associating with Communists or pro-Communist organizations."

Bitter at his treatment, Chaplin did not appeal the decision and settled in Switzerland, only visiting America again in 1972 to receive an honorary Oscar.

Charlie Chaplin (*foreground, second from left*) and Joan Barry sit in court during Barry's paternity suit against the Hollywood star in December 1944. Despite blood tests proving that he wasn't the father of her child, Chaplin lost the case.

For refusing to answer questions before the House Committee on Un-American Activities on the grounds that it would violate his First Amendment right to free speech, musician Pete Seeger was indicted for contempt of Congress in 1955.

KILLING SPREES

Young lovers on the run, stealing cars and shooting victims before a bloody denouement with the law—that was Bonnie Parker and Clyde Barrow in the early 1930s, right? Well, it could have been, but in the 1950s it was also nineteen-year-old Charles Starkweather and his fourteen-year-old girlfriend, Caril Ann Fugate. Between November 1957 and January 1958, Starkweather killed eleven people in Nebraska and Wyoming, beginning with a service station attendant who had refused to give him credit, before he turned on Fugate's mother and stepfather, and even her two-year-old half-sister. Then, when Fugate joined Starkweather, the couple went on a killing spree, shooting people as they stole money and cars. When they were caught, Starkweather was sent to the electric chair, while Fugate, who has always maintained her innocence, served seventeen years of a life sentence.

Young, in love, and stylish outlaws Bonnie Parker and Clyde Barrow captured the popular imagination in the early 1930s.

Strangely, for such a sordid story, Starkweather and Fugate captured the popular imagination in a romantic way. The 1973 film *Badlands* is loosely inspired by their story, while the two are the subject of Bruce Springsteen's 1982 song "Nebraska." Similarly, Bonnie and Clyde, who robbed grocery stores and killed thirteen people before being gunned down by police in Louisiana in 1934, have been celebrated in song and on film, most prominently in a 1967 movie starring Faye Dunaway and Warren Beatty. Benefiting from attractive photographs reproduced in newspapers, Bonnie and Clyde's story resonated with Depression-era readers. Here, it seemed, was a couple fighting back against an uncaring system, even if the people they were robbing were hardly doing much better than they were. They were the ultimate outsiders.

BONNIE AND CLYDE'S STORY OF OUTSIDERS RESONATED WITH DEPRESSION-ERA READERS.

But perhaps there is another element to the appeal of these crime couples. Is it that violence, guns, and riding off into the wilderness are part of the myth of America? Rather than a cowboy with a horse, it becomes a thief with a car, alone against the world—except perhaps for a lover caught up in a *folie à deux*.

Just as the myth of the violent-but-just cowboy in an unjust land is attractive, so the murderous pair are recast as desperate individuals fighting against an unfair system. The idea carries something of America's frontier spirit with it into the modern age.

Christianity." Just as communist governments were oppressing Catholics in Poland, Czechoslovakia, and Hungary, the anti-communist purges in America generated the fervor of religious persecution. Often described as witch hunts, once you were under suspicion for communist sympathies, it was very hard to prove your innocence. One method was to become an informer, naming colleagues or former friends, as a way of shifting the blame and throwing attention elsewhere. In a political climate pitched as capitalism vs. communism, good vs. evil, the simplistic rabble-rousing of McCarthyism was able to flourish.

THE BLACKLIST

People working in the film, radio, and television industry who had been accused of communist sympathies—however inaccurately—quickly found themselves blacklisted. The writer Dorothy Parker had had a series of Hollywood commissions throughout the 1940s, but her work for the studios dried up in 1950 when her name appeared in the *Red Channels* pamphlet listing 151 people of questionable loyalty to America. In all, it is estimated that more than 300 people were blacklisted in Hollywood and 1,500 in television and radio.

In 1955, folk singer Pete Seeger refused before HUAC to name personal and political associations on the grounds that this would violate his First Amendment rights to free speech. Indicted for Contempt of Congress, he had, for some years, to notify federal authorities when he planned to leave the Southern District of New York. American culture had benefited in the 1930s from new immigrants who had fled Nazi Germany, such as conductor Otto Klemperer, filmmaker Billy Wilder and actor Peter Lorre. But the persecution during America's anti-communist years generated traffic in the opposite direction. Klemperer's left-wing views led to his American passport not being renewed, and he moved to West Germany in 1954. Blacklisted American film directors Joseph

Losey and Jules Dassin left America for good, establishing new careers in Europe.

MCCARTHY'S FALL

Like the Salem witch trials of the 1690s, the mounting hysteria whipped up by Senator McCarthy only stopped when the inquisitors overreached themselves by targeting the establishment. With Salem the magistrates ceased being credulous when accusations were made against a senior churchman; similarly, when McCarthy suggested that there were communists in the US Army, the military was well able to fight back against his demagoguery.

With growing ill feeling among the public and politicians towards McCarthy, in 1954 he was censured by the Senate. By then an alcoholic, he was largely ignored politically, dying three years later. Although McCarthy fell from favor, the spirit of the time, of guilt by suspicion, lasted throughout the 1950s and, in some cases, into the 1970s, before burning out.

COVERT OPERATIONS

While on the one hand the US was developing ever-larger long-range nuclear weapons, on the other it was beginning to explore secretive work that did not require a nuclear arsenal or even troops on the ground. Formed in 1947, the Central Intelligence Agency (CIA) helped, in 1953, to topple the Mossadegh government in Iran, which had threatened Western access to its oil supplies. The following year, the CIA trained a five hundred-strong "Liberation Army" in Guatemala to overthrow the democratically elected socialist government of Jacobo Arbenz, whose reform programs challenged the interests of America's United Fruit Company. Landing in the American ambassador's plane, exiled Colonel Carlos Castillo Armas then seized power. His rule may have suited the interests of the United Fruit Company, but Armas

Critics of Senator McCarthy accused him of demagoguery, baseless defamation, and mudslinging, while he claimed that "McCarthyism is Americanism with its sleeves rolled." By 1954, he had lost political and popular support and was censured by the Senate.

imprisoned thousands of political opponents, ended secret ballots and disenfranchised three-quarters of the electorate. After three years in charge, he was assassinated.

Neither Mossadegh's or Arbenz's had been communist governments, but during the Cold War the fight would be broadened to include countries that it was feared might fall prey to communism, as well as those that were anti-Western.

THE SPACE RACE

With only 7 percent of the world's population, America, in 1950, accounted for half of its manufacturing production. But, in October 1957, it suffered a severe shock to its self-confidence when the Soviet Union beat the US into space with the launch of the first satellite, Sputnik 1. The following month, in Sputnik 2, Laika became the first dog in space. In response, Eisenhower immediately established NASA (National Aeronautics and Space Agency), while the 1958 National Defense Education Act ensured federal support for the teaching of math and science in schools. The 1960s would see the results of America's efforts to catch up in space.

Laika became the first animal to go into orbit when she was launched in the Soviet Sputnik 2 in November 1957. In 2002, it was admitted that she had died just a few hours into the mission.

THE WAR OF NERVES

Although America had become involved in Korea, it had not stepped in when French-Indochina fell to communist rule in 1954, nor, despite condemning the action, when Soviet forces invaded Hungary after the 1956 uprising. That would have risked direct confrontation with Moscow, and no one wanted that. The Cold War would, however, last for the next 30 years with different levels of intensity.

The following decade would see open fighting and near nuclear war between the countries of the East and those of the West, but there was mounting tension at home, too—that between black and white.

CHAPTER 3

THE CIVIL RIGHTS MOVEMENT

ALTHOUGH FULL CITIZENSHIP HAD BEEN GRANTED TO AFRICAN-Americans after the Civil War, subsequent state laws in the South had ensured that black people remained second-class citizens. Almost a century later, the civil rights movement would endure violence and killings before segregation and discrimination were made illegal.

With rifles ready and bayonets fixed, more than 1,000 paratroopers surrounded the building. A crowd of 1,500 people gathered. One man tried to grab a soldier's rifle and was knocked to the ground. Seven people were arrested.

Crowds? Paratroopers? What could have been causing such a commotion? Nothing more than nine teenagers attempting to enter their new school. These were not celebrity children (not yet) and this was not a special school—it was the Central High School in Little Rock, Arkansas. But the teenagers were black, and until that term in September 1957 the school had been for white children only.

The 250,000-strong, racially mixed crowd outside the Lincoln Memorial in Washington, DC, in August 1963, listen to Martin Luther King Jr. calling for racial equality and justice in his "I Have a Dream" speech.

Escorted by the paratroopers, the teenagers were able to begin their first desegregated high school classes. But was it really necessary to send paratroopers to protect them? Couldn't the police or the National Guard have ensured their safety? Well, no, they couldn't, or wouldn't, because three weeks earlier the same children had been blocked from enrolling at Central High *by* the National Guard.

As was shown repeatedly across the 1950s and 1960s, desegregation—whether of schools or elsewhere in society—was not solely a race issue. Like so much of the history of America in the previous century, it illustrated conflict—not only between the authority of the federal government and that of individual states, but also between attitudes in the North and South.

BEFORE THE CIVIL RIGHTS MOVEMENT

The Jim Crow segregation laws that had been introduced by the southern states at the beginning of the twentieth century—which decreed separate lunch counters and drinking fountains for black people and white people, as well as ruling that African-Americans had to board buses by the rear door and give up their seat to a white person if the bus became crowded—were still in place after World War II. Black people were also often denied voting rights in the south, where state laws made it difficult for them to register. In some places it wasn't simply a case of sending off a form: for a black person, voting often meant visiting the registration office in the few, possibly inconvenient, hours when it was open each month, and then having to answer obscure questions. In Alabama one such question was: "If the President does not wish to sign a bill, how many days is he allowed in which to return it to Congress for reconsideration?" Unsurprisingly, in Alabama and Mississippi in the early 1960s, less than 10 percent of the black population of voting age was registered.

In 1947, Jackie Robinson joined the Brooklyn Dodgers, becoming the first African American to play on a Major League Baseball team.

SMALL STEPS

Since the 1930s there had been improvements across the country as a whole for African Americans. For instance, in 1932, the Supreme Court ruled that black defendants on trial for life must have adequate legal presentation; in 1946, the Committee on Civil Rights recommended legislation against discrimination in jobs and voting, as well as a federal anti-lynching law; and two years later the armed forces were desegregated. In 1947, Jackie Robinson became the first African American to play in a Major League Baseball team, opening the door for others to follow.

The population was changing, too. While in 1910, 90 percent of black people lived in the South, by the 1960s, half lived in the North; overall, the African American population was now more urban than rural. The poor, however, remained disproportionately nonwhite, and the rising expectations of black people intensified resentment against racial subjugation in the South, as well as discrimination in the North. "Race," writes historian David Reynolds, "remained America's Achilles heel, the worm in its rosy apple of prosperity."

SCHOOL DAYS

In 1896, the Supreme Court had permitted the segregation of pupils into black and white schools under the decree that facilities be "separate but equal." But with equality being left to individual states to ensure, black schools in the south had become distinctly unequal. In 1954, following the efforts of the National Association for the Advancement of Colored People (NAACP), led by black lawyer Thurgood Marshall, the Supreme Court heard a case regarding segregation in Kansas's schools. It ruled that even if schools were equal, segregation on race "generates a feeling of inferiority" in the pupils, and concluded that "separate educational facilities are inherently unequal." To many, this sounded like a new birth of the freedom that had been promised after the Civil War. To some segregationists, however, it was "socialist doctrine," representing how the federal government had, in the words of Judge Tom Brady of Mississippi, "usurped the sacred privilege and right of respective states of this union to educate its youth." In his argument, it wasn't a matter or race, but political authority.

Just as equality in segregated schools had been left to the individual states to enforce, so now it would be up to the southern political elite to see that schools were desegregated. The Supreme Court may have made its ruling, but politicians weren't going to hurry it along if they didn't have to.

TO MANY, DESEGREGATING SCHOOLS SOUNDED LIKE THE NEW BIRTH OF THE FREEDOM THAT HAD BEEN PROMISED AFTER THE CIVIL WAR.

Desegregating schools in the South. The first black pupils at Little Rock Central High School, Arkansas, leaving the school under escort from paratroopers in 1957.

Even President Eisenhower admitted privately that he thought the Supreme Court's decision "set back progress in the South at least 15 years" and that to force desegregation was "just plain nuts." But, while the politicians were dragging their feet, African Americans were taking a stand.

BACK OF THE BUS

On Thursday December 1, 1955, Rosa Parks, a forty-two-year-old seamstress in Montgomery, Alabama, ignored a driver's order to give up her bus seat to a white person. Consequently, Parks, who was also secretary of the Montgomery chapter of the NAACP, was arrested and charged under Montgomery's segregation laws. She later explained her action as a way of finding out "what rights I had as a human being and a citizen."

When Parks was bailed the following evening by the president of Montgomery's NAACP, it was decided to use her case to protest against segregation. On the day of her trial, a bus boycott among African Americans was observed across the city. That same day, the Montgomery Improvement Association was formed, electing as its leader twenty-six-year-old Martin Luther King Jr. Highly educated, with a PhD from Boston University, King had been raised in Georgia before becoming a minister in Montgomery. From his first speech, he called for nonviolent protest against oppression. "In our protests there will be no cross burnings," he said, in reference to the Ku Klux Klan, "no white person will be taken from his home by a hooded Negro mob and brutally murdered." King reminded the crowd that the law—federal law, at least—was already on their side: "If we are wrong, the Supreme Court of this nation is wrong. If we are wrong, the Constitution of the United States is wrong." A nonviolent protest, the bus boycott—which had originally been planned for a single day—continued. Over time, the bus company and local businesses began to feel the pinch. Not that in the following weeks there wasn't violence *against* black people. There was, and it included the shattering of the front of King's house by a bomb. Nevertheless, a case

Rosa Parks has her fingerprints taken after being arrested for defying segregation laws in the Montgomery bus boycott in Montgomery, Alabama, in December 1955.

against segregated buses made its way through the courts. The following November, the Supreme Court declared Montgomery's segregated buses unconstitutional. Peaceful protest and legal doggedness had worked. In all, the bus boycott had lasted more than a year, but by Christmas 1956, Montgomery had ended segregation on its transport system. Encouraged, African Americans in other southern cities began bus boycotts.

THE LITTLE ROCK NINE

The events at Central High School in Little Rock, Arkansas, came nine months after the desegregation of Montgomery's buses. Despite an order from the Federal District Court to desegregate the schools, the governor of that state, Orval Faubus, had blocked integration, arguing that if he did, "blood would run in the streets," and that he was therefore acting to preserve the peace. So when the nine black teenagers arrived for their first day at the school on September 4, Faubus sent the National Guard to block their path. A crowd of more than four hundred white men and women gathered, some shouting hurtful racial slurs. Giving up, the teenagers went home.

Race, though, was not the only issue here; class played a role, too. In Little Rock, there were other high schools, some in wealthier areas, but it was only Central High, which catered for mainly working-class families, that had been selected for desegregation. Amis Guthridge, spokesman of the anti-desegregation Capital Citizens' Council, whipped up resentment, telling poor white people that the rich were making sure "the only race-mixing that is going to be done is in the districts where the so-called rednecks live." His point was that poor white people had most to fear economically and socially from black social mobility. Governor Faubus's act in blocking integration was one of defiance against the Supreme Court. When he wouldn't back down,

WHILE THE POLITICIANS WERE DRAGGING THEIR FEET, BLACK AMERICANS WERE TAKING A STAND.

President Eisenhower went over his head, sent in the paratroopers and federalized Arkansas's ten thousand-strong National Guard. The black pupils went to school, but their troubles were not over. Often racially abused by other pupils, one was suspended after she tipped food over a pupil who had been taunting her, only to be later expelled. The others, however, managed to complete the school year.

The following year it was decided to close all four of Little Rock's public schools in order to avoid a repeat of the situation. It would take a Supreme Court decision to reopen them.

Protesters hold placards reading "Race Mixing Is Communism" and "Stop the Race Mixing March of the Anti-Christ." They protest school desegregation outside the capitol building in Little Rock, Arkansas, in 1959.

NONVIOLENT PROTESTS

Further black protest came in the form of sit-ins staged across the South in 1960 to 1961. Taking their lead from Mahatma Gandhi's nonviolent action, black groups such as the Congress on Racial Equality (CORE) and Martin Luther King's Southern Christian Leadership Conference (SCLC) were well organized, with young members, both black and white, preparing for protests by role-playing what they would do and say when provoked.

Globally, they were encouraged, too—in 1960 alone, sixteen African countries gained their independence from European nations. "They were getting their freedom," said John Lewis, one of the founders of the Student Nonviolent Coordinating Committee (SNCC), "and we still didn't have ours in what we believed was a free country."

College students at a lunch counter sit-in, in Little Rock, Arkansas, in January 1962. The civil rights movement was characterized by nonviolent protest, such as sit-ins and marches.

FREEDOM RIDES

Again, federal law would prove to be at odds with state practices. In 1960, the Supreme Court ruled that segregation on interstate buses and trains was unconstitutional. This, however, was not being enforced—the new administration of President John F. Kennedy, who had been elected by a very small margin in 1960, being unwilling to risk alienating southern Democrats opposed to desegregation.

THE KU KLUX KLAN WAS REBORN AND OTHER WHITE VIGILANTE GROUPS WERE ESTABLISHED.

Passengers, including Freedom Riders sponsored by the Congress of Racial Equality (CORE), escape their Greyhound bus after it has been set on fire by whites opposed to the desegregation of interstate buses in May 1961.

A hundred years after Lincoln's Emancipation Proclamation, "the life of the Negro is still sadly crippled by the manacles of segregation and the chains of discrimination" says Martin Luther King Jr. in his "I Have a Dream" speech in Washington, DC, in August 1963.

Activists such as James Farmer of CORE realized that, in order to win, they had to make it more dangerous for the federal government *not* to enforce federal law than to enforce it. To achieve this, they would, in a nonviolent way, provoke violence, thus embarrassing the government into taking action. This helped broaden the issue beyond local legislation and state politics. Beginning in May 1961, Freedom Rides involved pairs of volunteers—one white, one black—who would board interstate buses, with the black volunteer refusing to move from a seat at the front and the white volunteer sitting at the back. In addition, in waiting rooms, the black volunteers would try to use the whites-only facilities. As anticipated, some of the volunteers were beaten up and jailed, and several buses were even firebombed. Although President Kennedy tried to calm the situation, violence against Freedom Riders continued. But within five months of the Freedom Rides beginning, the Interstate Commerce Commission announced that all buses and terminals must display signs announcing that all seating was desegregated. Direct action had won.

Violence, however, would continue. The Ku Klux Klan was reborn and other white vigilante groups were established. In 1962, the prospect of a black student being admitted to the University of Mississippi sparked a campus riot that had to be suppressed by federal troops, with Mississippi's National Guard being brought under federal control. In June 1963, black civil rights activist Medgar Evers was assassinated in Jackson, Mississippi, while in Birmingham, Alabama, four children were killed in the bombing of a black church.

To those who criticized direct action, Martin Luther King responded with these words in 1963: "We have waited for more than 340 years for our constitutional and God-given rights. The nations of Asia and Africa are moving with jet-like speed toward the goal of political independence, and we still creep at horse-and-buggy pace toward the gaining of a cup of coffee at a lunch counter."

Marches and sit-ins kept the issue in the headlines. In August 1963, King's march on Washington culminated in his "I Have a Dream" speech delivered on the steps of the Lincoln Memorial to a crowd of around 250,000 people. Following this, Kennedy proposed a new civil rights bill. The bill hadn't got far before Kennedy was assassinated in November, but his successor, Lyndon B. Johnson, pushed it through, even telling Congress that it would be a fitting way to honor JFK's memory. The Civil Rights Act, signed by Johnson in July 1964, made illegal all forms of segregation and discrimination.

FREEDOM SUMMER

The obstructive voting regulations against black people, however, remained in place, so volunteers, both black and white, including many student activists, set out to increase voter registration. Protesting in Selma, Alabama, in January 1965, King was jailed, along with many teachers and their schoolchildren; when, two months later, protesters tried to take their case to the state capital in Montgomery, state troopers barred their way, before mounted police attacked.

Two weeks later, King led a large crowd on the 50-mile (80 km) march from Selma to Montgomery. When Alabama's governor George Wallace—who had declared in his inaugural address two years earlier "segregation now, segregation tomorrow, segregation forever"—refused to provide protection for the marchers, President Johnson overruled him by federalizing the National Guard and sending in the US Army. The following week, Johnson asked Congress for a voting rights act by which the federal government would be able to eliminate all local and state obstacles to voting for black people. The act was signed that August; within three years, black registration to vote had reached 60 percent of potential voters in Mississippi and Alabama.

Ratified in the Fourteenth Amendment in 1868, full citizenship had been left to the liberty of the states to enforce. Now, ninety-seven years later, the freedom of those states *not to enforce* had been overridden by the federal government.

In Selma, Alabama, in March 1965, police attack civil rights activists attempting to march to Montgomery to protest racial discrimination in voter registration.

THE WATTS RIOTS

In August 1965, Watts, a black area in Los Angeles, erupted into racial violence. Beginning with a minor event—after white police arrested a black man for drunk driving—the situation escalated into riots. After six days of burning and looting, thirty-four African Americans were dead. Among some of those responsible for the rioting, there was some sense of satisfaction. Not only had they kicked back at the police, whom they regarded as racist, they had also drawn attention to the causes of their unrest.

AFTER SIX DAYS OF BURNING AND LOOTING, THIRTY-FOUR BLACK PEOPLE WERE DEAD.

While there was no segregation in Los Angeles or elsewhere outside the South, there was still discrimination. Black people were more likely to be unemployed or in lower-level work, while they often paid more for housing than white people. Where in its earlier years the civil rights movement had been most active in the South, in the mid-1960s racial conflict intensified in other cities in other states, police violence against the black community often being blamed for provoking riots. Protesting in 1966 against Chicago's discrimination of its one million black people in the housing market, Martin Luther King was shocked at the reception they received in middle-class white suburbs—with Nazi flags, bottles being lobbed, and taunts being spat at civil rights supporters. "I have never seen," said King, "even in Mississippi and Alabama, mobs as hostile and hate-filled as I've seen in Chicago."

Police search African American youth in the Los Angeles district of Watts in March 1966, during the second race riot in eight months. While there was no segregation in Los Angeles, there was still discrimination.

MISSISSIPPI BURNING

Because southern states still had unjust policies that blocked many African Americans from registering to vote, civil rights activists did what they could to fight for equality at the polls. In Longdale, Mississippi, in late May 1964, two such activists—James Chaney, a twenty-one-year-old black Mississippian, and Michael Schwerner, a twenty-four-year-old white New Yorker—spoke at Mount Zion Methodist Church about opening a freedom school to help the congregation pass the literacy requirements to register to vote.

Learning of the freedom school idea, members of the Mississippi White Knights, a Ku Klux Klan splinter group, hatched a plan to rid the area of the two activists. To lure Chaney and Schwerner back to Longdale, twenty-four armed Klansmen burned down Mount Zion Methodist Church. This worked; on June 21, Schwerner and Chaney, joined by Andrew Goodman, a twenty-year-old white New Yorker, returned to the town to see what had happened.

Driving out of Longdale that evening, the three were followed by twenty-six-year-old deputy sheriff and White Knights member Cecil R. Price, who stopped them before escorting them to a secluded junction. There, a car of seven Klansmen joined Price. Chaney was beaten and shot three times, while Schwerner and Goodman were each shot once in the heart. The bodies were buried in an earth dam. From the red clay later found in Goodman's lungs, it appeared that he had been buried alive.

When the three men were reported missing, the FBI launched a major manhunt. The activists' bodies were found several weeks later on the strength of a tip by an FBI informant, later revealed to be a local highway patrolman. In the ensuing investigation, many suspects were identified, with James Jordan and another conspirator confessing their roles. But Mississippi officials refused to prosecute for murder—a state crime. The eighteen men whom the FBI had identified were charged with conspiring to deprive the activists of their civil rights—the only way they could be tried under federal government authority.

After legal wrangling, the trial began in Meridian, Mississippi, in October 1967. Seven of the men were found guilty, including Price, with sentences ranging from three to ten years. Having become a major prosecution witness, James Jordan was tried separately, receiving a four-year sentence.

But the convictions weren't over. With the jury reaching a deadlock over the case against Edgar Ray Killen, a preacher whom, it is believed, planned and directed the killings, but who had not carried out the shootings, the judge decided not to retry him. Only in June 2005, forty years after the killings, was he retried, with a jury convicting him on three counts of manslaughter. When he was interviewed in prison in December 2014, Killen said that he remained a segregationist and did not believe in racial equality.

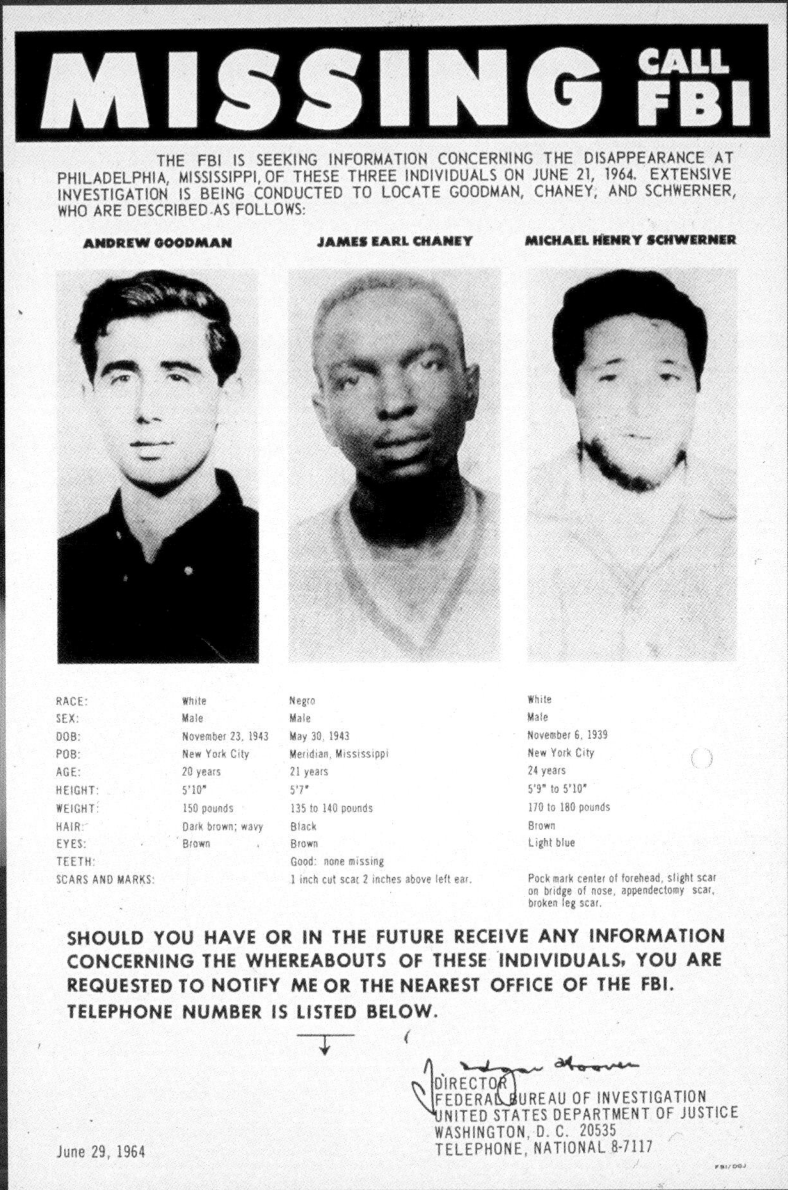
MISSING CALL FBI

THE FBI IS SEEKING INFORMATION CONCERNING THE DISAPPEARANCE AT PHILADELPHIA, MISSISSIPPI, OF THESE THREE INDIVIDUALS ON JUNE 21, 1964. EXTENSIVE INVESTIGATION IS BEING CONDUCTED TO LOCATE GOODMAN, CHANEY, AND SCHWERNER, WHO ARE DESCRIBED AS FOLLOWS:

	ANDREW GOODMAN	JAMES EARL CHANEY	MICHAEL HENRY SCHWERNER
RACE:	White	Negro	White
SEX:	Male	Male	Male
DOB:	November 23, 1943	May 30, 1943	November 6, 1939
POB:	New York City	Meridian, Mississippi	New York City
AGE:	20 years	21 years	24 years
HEIGHT:	5'10"	5'7"	5'9" to 5'10"
WEIGHT:	150 pounds	135 to 140 pounds	170 to 180 pounds
HAIR:	Dark brown; wavy	Black	Brown
EYES:	Brown	Brown	Light blue
TEETH:		Good: none missing	
SCARS AND MARKS:		1 inch cut scar 2 inches above left ear.	Pock mark center of forehead, slight scar on bridge of nose, appendectomy scar, broken leg scar.

SHOULD YOU HAVE OR IN THE FUTURE RECEIVE ANY INFORMATION CONCERNING THE WHEREABOUTS OF THESE INDIVIDUALS, YOU ARE REQUESTED TO NOTIFY ME OR THE NEAREST OFFICE OF THE FBI. TELEPHONE NUMBER IS LISTED BELOW.

DIRECTOR
FEDERAL BUREAU OF INVESTIGATION
UNITED STATES DEPARTMENT OF JUSTICE
WASHINGTON, D. C. 20535
TELEPHONE, NATIONAL 8-7117

June 29, 1964

FBI/DOJ

The murdered civil rights activists (*left to right*) Andrew Goodman, James Chaney, and Michael Schwerner.

While providing helpful community social programs, the Black Panthers, members of which are shown above during a protest, were a revolutionary organization, calling not for integration but black separatism—and they were not opposed to violence.

There were further riots in Detroit and Newark in 1967. Some commentators pointed to agitators or communist manipulation as the cause, but an investigation by the Presidential Commission found poverty, unemployment, and improper police practices to be factors. Black people made up about 10 percent of the American population, but constituted almost one-third of those living below the poverty line.

In the spring of 1968, violence erupted in more than 100 cities. This had a very precise trigger: on April 4, while standing on a hotel balcony in Memphis, Tennessee, Martin Luther King was shot dead by white petty criminal James Earl Ray.

BLACK POWER

By the time of Martin Luther King's death, his nonviolent protests and ideas of integration had lost some ground to new black movements. Activist Stokely Carmichael was now calling for more direct confrontation. On release after his twenty-seventh arrest in June 1966, he addressed a crowd of three thousand people in Mississippi: "We been saying "freedom" for six years and we ain't got nothin'. What we gonna start saying now is Black Power!"

This wasn't the first time the term "Black Power" had been heard, but it now began to take hold, and it marked a turning point in the civil rights movement. While Carmichael never resorted to violence, at times his rhetoric seemed likely to provoke it. "When you talk of Black Power, you talk of building a movement that will smash everything that Western civilization has created," he said. Having worked closely with white activists in groups such as the Student Nonviolent Coordinating Committee, many black activists now became increasingly extremist and combative.

IN THE SPRING OF 1968, VIOLENCE ERUPTED IN MORE THAN 100 CITIES.

More extreme, the Black Panther movement was formed that October in San Francisco. Theirs was a revolutionary manifesto, when, at the

Boxer Muhammad Ali speaking to the press outside the United Nations building in New York in March 1964, with (*wearing glasses*) the Nation of Islam's Malcolm X.

STONEWALL RIOTS

The civil rights movement prompted other groups to push for similar rights. With homosexual acts still criminalized in all states (other than Illinois in 1962), few establishments welcomed openly gay people. The Stonewall Inn in Greenwich Village, New York, became popular among some of the city's most marginalized residents, with its customers including drag queens, transgender people, and male prostitutes. Police raids on gay bars were common, but, during one at the Stonewall in June 1969, the customers fought back, the bar went up in flames, and over the next few days there were riots in the neighborhood. The following month, the Gay Liberation Front was formed, and, during the next year, other gay rights groups were established, with the first Gay Pride march marking the anniversary of the Stonewall Riots. From the 1970s, states began to decriminalize homosexual acts, with the Supreme Court invalidating all remaining laws against homosexuality in 2003.

height of the Vietnam War, they sought common cause with Vietnamese communists. Further, calling not for integration but for black separatism, they were prepared to use guns to try to achieve their goals. Although the movement did some worthwhile social work, it also became tainted and bloodied by drug trafficking, bank robberies, rape, and murder. By the end of the decade the Black Panthers—and their armed wing, the Black Liberation Army—had been destroyed by the police and FBI.

The separatist black Muslim movement known as the Nation of Islam had built support in urban ghettos from the 1950s, before raising its profile to a national level through the oratory skills of its leader, Malcolm X. Born Malcolm Little, he had changed his surname to symbolize the African family name of the slave ancestor that he would never know. For a time, Malcolm X was considered a firebrand, until, gradually moving

People gather outside the Stonewall Inn in New York following the riots that erupted there between the gay community and police in June 1969.

to a more racially tolerant position, he became alienated from the sectarian views of the leadership of the Nation of Islam. He was assassinated by three of its members in 1965. Perhaps the best-known supporter of the Nation of Islam was Muhammad Ali. His name, too, tells a story of African American history. Born Cassius Clay, he was named after his father Cassius Marcellus Clay Sr., who, in turn, had been named after a white nineteenth-century slave abolitionist and politician. In 1964, having just become world heavyweight champion, Clay joined the Nation of Islam, changing his name to Cassius X and then, later, Muhammad Ali. "His transition from being a white clone into a symbol of black pride and then of radical separatism was a parable of sixties' America," writes historian David Reynolds. Although in later years Ali would step back from his early calls for separatism and become something of a beacon for peaceful relations between the races, he remained a Muslim until his death in 2016.

SIGN OF THE TIMES

By the mid-1960s, the civil rights movement had achieved immense change in making segregation and discrimination illegal, while stirring other rights movements. But there had also been associated mob violence, murders, and assassinations. America, however, was already involved in a foreign war, and more assassinations were to come in what would be a tumultuous decade.

GLOSSARY

activist A person who supports or exercises direct action on the side of controversial issues, known as activism.

Cold War A conflict, though, unlike a physical war in that it is carried on by methods short of sustained overt military action and usually without compromising peace or diplomacy, such as the Cold War between the United States and the USSR.

D-Day Referring to June 6, 1944, when the Allies began to invade German-occupied France during World War II.

demagoguery A practice in which a leader manipulates prejudice, misconception, and general falseness to achieve power and influence over a people.

denouement The result of a series of complex events, or, the result of the overarching events of a literary work or story.

Holocaust Referring to the imprisonment and mass killing of Jews and other Europeans by the Nazi Party in World War II.

internment To be held as a prisoner for political, military, or social motivations in a confined area, such as the Japanese American internment camps during World War II.

McCarthyism Named for Joseph R. McCarthy during the heightened fear of communism in America, McCarthyism is the method of accusing a person or group of people of crimes, such as treason or espionage, without due evidence to the claim.

National Association for the Advancement of Colored People (NAACP) A US civil rights organization formed in 1909 to ensure the fair treatment and equal opportunity of African Americans.

Red Scare An instance or period in which a fear of communism or leftist ideals is encouraged and manipulated, particularly referring to the Cold War period of heightened paranoia in the United States.

segregation When a law or laws separate aspects of infrastructure, education, and overall society by race, ethnicity, class, or other defining characteristics of prejudice.

separatism Any belief in or support for an event of separation, such as cultural separatism.

Stonewall Riots A series of protests by the gay community against a police raid at the Stonewall Inn in New York City, cited as one of the most important beginnings of the LGBTQ+ movement in the United States.

FOR MORE INFORMATION

Canadian Museum for Human Rights
85 Israel Asper Way
Winnipeg, Manitoba R3C 0L5
Canada
(204) 289-2000
Website: *https://humanrights.ca/home*
This museum discusses not only the essential past, but also the necessary future of human rights, examining important events such as the Holocaust and educating visitors on changing perspectives and human-rights violations today.

Diefenbunker Museum—Canada's Cold War Museum
3929 Carp Rd,
Carp, ON K0A 1L0, Canada
(613) 839-0007
Website: *http://diefenbunker.ca/*
The four-story, 100,000 square foot bunker was built during the Cold War to house Canadian officials and officers in a nuclear event, which has since been turned into an interactive museum open to the public for the purpose of retelling the Cold War.

The International Museum of World War II
8 Mercer Road
Natick, MA 01760
(508) 651-1944
Website: *https://museumofworldwarii.org/*
This museum boasts more than half a million artifacts and exhibits devoted to telling the full story of the Axis and Allied powers.

National Association for the Advancement of Colored People (NAACP)
4805 Mt. Hope Drive
Baltimore MD 21215
Local: (410) 580-5777
Website: *http://www.naacp.org/*
The NAACP exists to fight and eliminate race-based discrimination and promote equality in all aspects of society.

National Civil Rights Museum
450 Mulberry Street
Memphis, TN 38103
(901) 521-9699
Website: *http://www.civilrightsmuseum.org*
This museum lets visitors learn through important artifacts, multisensory media, and interactive experiences that give hands-on accounts on the history and relevance of the civil rights movement.

World War Two Studies Association
Department of History, Kansas State University
208 Eisenhower Hall
Manhattan, KS, 66506-1002
(785)-532-3786
Website: *https://www.k-state.edu/history/institute/Partnerships/WWTSA.html*
Since 1967 the association has encouraged the study of all aspects and information relating to World War II.

FURTHER READING

Anderson, Devery S., and Julian Bond. *Emmett Till: The Murder That Shocked the World and Propelled the Civil Rights Movement* (Race, Rhetoric and Media). Jackson, MS: The University Press of Mississippi, 2015.

Bausum, Ann. *Stonewall: Breaking Out in the Fight for Gay Rights*. New York, NY: Viking Books for Young Readers, 2015.

Brands, H. W. *The General vs. the President: MacArthur and Truman at the Brink of Nuclear War*. New York, NY: Doubleday—Penguin Random House, LLC., 2016.

Engler, Mark, and Paul Engler. *This Is an Uprising: How Nonviolent Revolt is Shaping the Twenty-First Century*. New York, NY: Nation Book—Perseus Books Group, 2016.

Fischer, Nick. *Spider Web: The Birth of American Anticommunism*. Champaign, IL: University of Illinois Press, 2016.

Ivey, Linda L., and Kevin W. Kaatz. *Citizen Internees: A Second Look at Race and Citizenship in Japanese American Internment Camps*. Santa Barbara, CA: Praeger—ABC-CLIO, LLC., 2017.

Michaels, Jonathan. *McCarthyism: The Realities, Delusions and Politics Behind the 1950s Red Scare* (Critical Moments in American History). New York, NY: Routledge—Taylor & Francis Group, 2017.

Rupprecht, Tobias. *Soviet Internationalism after Stalin: Interaction and Exchange between the USSR and Latin America during the Cold War.* Cambridge, CB2 8BS, UK: Cambridge University Press, 2015.

Schmidli, William Michael. *The Fate of Freedom Elsewhere: Human Rights and U.S. Cold War Policy toward Argentina*. Ithaca, NY: Cornell University Press, 2013.

Simpson, Kevin E. *Soccer under the Swastikas: Stories of Survival and Resistance during the Holocaust*. Lanham, MD: Rowman & Littlefield Publishers, 2016.

INDEX

T

U

W